written by Sierra Wilson
illustrated by Nicole Koa

My Testimony Tree

CFI • An imprint of Cedar Fort, Inc. • Springville, Utah

My testimony is special.
It's the spiritual things I know.
And just like a tree,
every day it can grow.

My testimony started small,
much like a tiny seed.
With loving care
it grows each day
with slow and steady speed.

At first my tree was tiny,
with just a leaf or two.
I knew that Jesus loved me,
and Heavenly Father too.

My tree is growing bigger
as I tend it every day.
It sprouts new leaves when I feed it
as I study my scriptures and pray.

Choosing right and serving others
also help my tree grow tall.
When I do good, I feel the Spirit,
with a warmth that's still and small.

As I learn and follow Jesus,
I add branches to my tree.
I gain a testimony of prophets
and of eternal family.

But like a real tree,
my testimony can get sick
or even die.

It can shrivel up or shrink
if I forget to care and try.

Bad choices are like weeds
that choke my testimony tree.
When I repent and follow God,
I kill the weeds and feel so free.

But sometimes I'll still struggle.
I'll need help for my tree to stand.
Good friends, parents, teachers,
and my Savior will lend a hand.

And as my tree grows stronger,
I can help out others too.
I can share my testimony
of the things I know are true.

I'll work hard every day.

I'll always do my part.

I want my testimony's roots

deep inside my heart.

My testimony tree
may be small today,
but I know how to help it grow
bit by bit, day by day.

My tree is part of a big forest
with other trees tall and strong.
We keep our faith together
and help each other along.

Our trees grow the best fruits
like peace and joy and love.
All of these are precious gifts
from Heavenly Father above.

My testimony is special.
It's the spiritual things I know.
And just like a tree,
every day it can grow.

To my parents and Sis. Lowry, Sis. Cox, Sis. Ranc, and everyone who helped my testimony tree grow.

—Sierra

© 2022 Sierra Wilson
Illustrations © 2022 Nicole Koa
All rights reserved.

This is not an official publication of the Church of Jesus Christ of Latter-day Saints. The opinions and views expressed herein belong solely to the author and do not necessarily represent the opinions or views of Cedar Fort, Inc. Permission for the use of sources, graphics, and photos is also solely the responsibility of the author.

ISBN 13: 978-1-4621-3578-3

Published by CFI, an imprint of Cedar Fort, Inc.
2373 W. 700 S., Springville, UT 84663
Distributed by Cedar Fort, Inc., www.cedarfort.com

Library of Congress Control Number: 2020941182

Cover design by Shawnda T. Craig
Cover design © 2022 Cedar Fort, Inc.

Printed in the United States of America

10 9 8 7 6 5 4 3 2 1

Printed on acid-free paper